PIANO / VOCAL / GUITAR

# LANA DEL REY
# ULTRAVIOLENCE

ISBN 978-1-4950-0016-4

7777 W. BLUEMOUND RD. P.O. BOX 13819 MILWAUKEE, WI 53213

Visit Hal Leonard Online at
**www.halleonard.com**

# CRUEL WORLD

Words and Music by ELIZABETH GRANT
and BLAKE STRANATHAN

yeah. Be-cause you're young, you're wild, you're free, you're danc-in'

cir-cles a-round me. You're fuck-in' cra - zy. Oh,

oh, you're cra-zy for me.

1 I shared my

2 Got your Bi - ble and your gun.

You like your wom - en and you like fun. ___ I like my

can - dy and your her - o - in. ___ And I'm so hap - py, so hap - py now you're

gone. ___

**D.S. al Coda**

**CODA**

Oh, ___ oh, ___

___ you're cra - zy for ___ me.

# ULTRAVIOLENCE

Words and Music by ELIZABETH GRANT
and DANIEL HEATH

# SHADES OF COOL

Words and Music by ELIZABETH GRANT
and RICK NOWELS

# BROOKLYN BABY

Words and Music by ELIZABETH GRANT
and BARRIE O'NEILL

# WEST COAST

Words and Music by ELIZABETH GRANT
and RICK NOWELS

Down on the West Coast, ___
Down on the West Coast, ___

___ they got a say - in', "If you're not drink - in', then you're not play - in'." But you ___
___ they got their i - cons, their sil - ver star - lets, their Queens of Sai - gon. And you ___

# SAD GIRL

Words and Music by ELIZABETH GRANT
and RICK NOWELS

# PRETTY WHEN YOU CRY

Words and Music by ELIZABETH GRANT
and BLAKE STRANATHAN

*Recorded a half step lower.

# MONEY POWER GLORY

Words and Music by ELIZABETH GRANT
and GREG KURSTIN

*Recorded a half step higher.*

# FUCKED MY WAY TO THE TOP

Words and Music by ELIZABETH GRANT
and DANIEL HEATH

# OLD MONEY

Words and Music by ELIZABETH GRANT,
NINO ROTA, DANIEL HEATH
and ROBBIE FITZSIMMONS

*Recorded a half step lower.

# THE OTHER WOMAN

Words and Music by
JESSIE ROBINSON